Inventing the American Past:

THE ART OF F.O.C. DARLEY

American & Foreign

Portrait Gallery.

PROMINENT PORTRAITS.
No. 2876.

DARLEY, ARTIST—THE INIMITABLE.

PUBLISHED BY E. & H. T. ANTHONY & CO.
American and Foreign Stereoscopic Emporium, 501 Broadway, New York.

Inventing the American Past:
The Art of F.O.C. Darley

Nancy Finlay

The New York Public Library · 1999

Published for the exhibition *Inventing the American Past: The Art of F.O.C. Darley* presented at The New York Public Library, Humanities and Social Sciences Library, Stokes Gallery, April 17–June 26, 1999 and at Brandywine River Museum, Chadds Ford, Pennsylvania September 11–November 21, 1999

Copyright © 1999 by The New York Public Library, Astor, Lenox and Tilden Foundations
All rights reserved

The name "The New York Public Library" and the representation of the lion appearing in this work are registered marks and the property of The New York Public Library, Astor, Lenox and Tilden Foundations.

Library of Congress Cataloging-in-Publication Data
Finlay, Nancy.
    Inventing the American past : the art of F.O.C. Darley / Nancy Finlay.
        p.   cm.
    Published for the exhibition presented at the New York Public Library, Humanities and Social Sciences Library, Stokes Gallery, April 17–June 26, 1999 and at Brandywine River Museum, Chadds Ford, Pa., Sept. 11–Nov. 21, 1999.
    Includes bibliographical references.
    ISBN 0-87104-445-5
    1. Darley, Felix Octavius Carr, 1822–1888 — Exhibitions. 2. New York Public Library — Art collections — Exhibitions. I. Stokes Gallery. II. Brandywine River Museum. III. Title.
NC975.5.D37A4 1999   99-13745
741.6'4'092 — dc21   CIP

Printed on acid-free paper
Printed in the United States of America

On the cover: F.O.C. Darley, *Elisabeth Grace and Rachel Martin*. Preliminary drawing in graphite, black ink, and wash, ca. 1850 [Cat. No. 74, detail]

On the endpapers, left to right: *The Deerslayer* [Cat. No. 111]; *The Jack-Knife* [Cat. No. 110]; *Indian Hunting Buffalo* [Cat. No. 116]; *Surveyors* [Cat. No. 120]

Frontispiece: E. and H. T. Anthony, *Darley, Artist – The Inimitable*. Stereo photograph, ca. 1862? [Cat. No. 100]

Contents

Foreword, *by Roberta Waddell* · 7

Acknowledgments · 10

Inventing the American Past: The Art of F.O.C. Darley · 11

Checklist of the Exhibition · 38

Selected Bibliography · 51

Foreword

In 1909, the director of The New York Public Library advised the first Curator of Prints, Frank Weitenkampf, "It is desired that this print room contain as complete a collection as possible of the results of the graphic arts as practiced in America." In the previous century, the Lenox Library, one of the collections with which The New York Public Library was founded, housed many American prints, including such notable nineteenth-century graphic icons as James and James D. Smillie's print after Thomas Cole's *Voyage of Life* and Alfred Jones's engraving after Richard Caton Woodville's painting *Mexican News*, along with copious portraits of American heroes, particularly George Washington. By 1895, when its collections became part of The New York Public Library, the Lenox Library had become a notable repository of Americana; among the major gifts and purchases were the Emmet Collection, with its thousands of prints and some drawings illustrating the early history of this nation; the Bancroft Collection, which included a rare set of Amos Doolittle's engravings of the Battles of Lexington and Concord; the Ford Collection, with a selection of early American views and Paul Revere's engraved portrait of Jonathan Mayhew; and the Duyckinck Collection, including a fine collection of English and American nineteenth-century illustrated books.

Even before these collections moved in 1911 to the grand Carrère & Hastings building on Fifth Avenue, which now houses the Humanities and Social Sciences Library of The New York Public Library, and before Weitenkampf, the author of such basic texts as *The American Illustrator, American Graphic Art*, and *Political Caricature in the United States*, was officially directed to build the American holdings, he was committed to American prints and book illustration. Shortly after the Print Collection was established in 1900, he welcomed gifts of prints by members of the American Etching Revival from the esteemed New York print dealer Frederick Keppel, along with several collections of late nineteenth-century American wood engravings, most of which had been commissioned for popular magazines. Some of these were given by magazine publishers, others by the brilliantly skilled wood engravers themselves. Weitenkampf encouraged such donations, and during the Print Collection's early, formative years, many American artists including John Sloan, "Pop" Hart, and Edward Hopper apparently responded to Weitenkampf's solicitations. Sometimes family members offered these gifts: James David Smillie gave a major collection of prints by his father, the nineteenth-century artist James Smillie (the son's prints came later as a bequest);

Mary Nimmo Moran's daughters presented the Library with a significant number of their mother's etchings; John Durand gave numerous prints, many in multiple states, by his father, the engraver-turned-painter Asher B. Durand; and by 1901, Jane Darley had made a generous gift of drawings by her late husband, F.O.C. Darley, as well as wood engravings made after his designs for book illustrations.

During the forty-two years of his stewardship, Weitenkampf continued to acquire contemporary American prints: Sloan and Hopper have been mentioned; George Bellows, John Marin, Childe Hassam, Rockwell Kent, the Soyer brothers, Martin Lewis, Peggy Bacon, Charles Sheeler, and Isabel Bishop are among the virtual Who's Who of American graphic artists whose work was bought by or given to the Print Collection. At the same time, great collections of earlier American prints were arriving at the Library. In 1915, David McNeely Stauffer, who wrote the landmark directory of American seventeenth-, eighteenth-, and nineteenth-century prints and printmakers, donated his collection. Two other gifts established the Library as a major repository of American historical views. In 1922, the Library received from Amos F. Eno nearly five hundred New York views recording the city's growth from the seventeenth through the nineteenth centuries; in 1930, I. N. Phelps Stokes donated some eight hundred American historical prints and early views of American cities. In 1943, shortly after Weitenkampf retired, the Library was given approximately 1,200 prints, all issued by the New York Graphic Arts Division of the Federal Art Project of the Works Progress Administration. As views from the Stokes and Eno collections recorded our country in the eighteenth and nineteenth centuries, the artists of the American rural and urban scene, and those enrolled in the WPA, provided an important record of life in the United States during the first half of this century.

The precedent set by Frank Weitenkampf has been sustained during the second half of this century; the Library continues its commitment "to assemble as complete a collection as possible . . . of the graphic arts as practiced in America," acquiring contemporary prints, illustrated books, and artist's books. Though often less literally descriptive than an eighteenth-century topographical view or a John Sloan etching of a New York City street in 1905, contemporary prints and illustrated books can, nevertheless, be telling recorders and cultural indicators that mirror and comment on our society. Much as Darley brilliantly gave visible reality to historical and fictional figures, as well as to contemporary nineteenth-century events, artists continue today to provide us with a way to view, interpret, and comprehend our culture and our times.

For much of this century, the Library's American print and illustrated book collections have been a rich resource for exhibitions and catalogues. But although F.O.C. Darley's drawings, prints, and illustrated books were a part of the Print Collection from its beginnings, Darley had never been the subject of a Library catalogue or exhibition. Nancy Finlay now redresses this omission and, drawing upon the Library's rich and often unique Darley holdings, documents the career of this important artist-illustrator, placing his work in the context of developments in nineteenth-century American graphic arts. In so doing, she not only establishes his significant place in the history of American art, she also vividly brings Darley to life, just as Darley himself, through his unforgettable illustrations, infused our history, legends, and lore with a convincing reality.

ROBERTA WADDELL
Curator of Prints
Miriam and Ira D. Wallach Division of Art, Prints and Photographs
The New York Public Library

February 1999

Acknowledgments

This exhibition has been made possible by the continuing generosity of Miriam and Ira D. Wallach. Funding for the catalogue was provided by Leonard L. Milberg, a longtime friend and loyal benefactor of The New York Public Library and its Print Collection and a passionate and knowledgeable scholar and collector of American historical prints.

Sue Welsh Reed, Martha Shiek, and Ray and Judith Hester all provided invaluable research assistance as well as encouragement and support throughout the lengthy evolution of the project. Many members of the staff of The New York Public Library, including Virginia Bartow, Miriam Mandelbaum, John Rathé, Mimi Bowling, Julia VanHaaften, Sharon Frost, and Rodney Phillips, were also helpful at various points during my research. Marilan Lund, Barbara Bergeron, and Karen Van Westering were responsible for the design and production of the catalogue; Barbara Suhr and her staff in the Exhibitions Program were responsible for the design and installation of the exhibition. Finally, profound thanks are due to Robert Rainwater, the Miriam and Ira D. Wallach Chief Librarian for Art, Prints and Photographs and Curator of the Spencer Collection, and to my former colleagues in the Library's Print Collection: Roberta Waddell, Margaret Glover, Radames Suarez, and Elizabeth Wyckoff. This catalogue and exhibition would never have come to be without their ongoing understanding, assistance, and support.

After I left The New York Public Library in June 1998, Roberta Waddell and Elizabeth Wyckoff assumed responsibility for the completion of the catalogue and the implementation of my plans for the exhibition; both the exhibition and the catalogue were possible only because of their willingness to see them through to completion. *Inventing the American Past: The Art of F.O.C. Darley* owes fully as much to their hard work as it does to mine; I would like to dedicate this publication to these two marvelous colleagues in recognition of their contribution to it.

NANCY FINLAY
Curator of Graphics
The Connecticut Historical Society

Inventing the American Past:

THE ART OF F.O.C. DARLEY

The United States was less than fifty years old at the time of F.O.C. Darley's birth in 1821,[1] and it was commonplace to lament the new nation's lack of myths, legends, and historical associations. Although some authors had begun to respond to the call for a national literature, and some artists had begun the attempt to create distinctly American art, book illustration remained a sadly neglected field. While editions of literary classics with illustrations by major artists were beginning to appear in Europe, American artists, struggling hard to establish their reputations in a country with little appreciation for the fine arts, avoided a field that traditionally had suffered from especially low esteem, far below even such despised genres as landscape and portrait painting. As a result, many illustrations in American books and periodicals were simply direct copies or crude adaptations of European originals. British artist John Flaxman's outline illustrations for Homer, Dante, Milton, and Bunyan began appearing in 1793, and were to exert a profound influence on Continental artists in the early decades of the nineteenth century. His imitators included the German artist Moritz Retzsch, who produced his own outline illustrations for works by Shakespeare, Schiller, and Goethe. Other European artists, employing different media and different styles, created equally monumental masterpieces of book illustration during this same period. John Martin's mezzotint illustrations for *Paradise Lost* were published in London between 1824 and 1828, and Eugène Delacroix's lithographs for Goethe's *Faust* appeared in Paris during the latter year. Until Darley came of age in the 1840s, however, no American illustrator emerged to challenge these European masters.

Darley's rise to fame was meteoric. Born in Philadelphia to parents who were both actors, he was originally destined for an unexciting but eminently respectable career as a clerk. It was probably his brother-in-law, the fashionable portrait painter Thomas Sully, who inspired his interest in the visual arts; in any case, his remarkable talent was evident at an early age. Even before he was twenty years old he was contributing designs to *Godey's Magazine* and other Philadelphia publications. Edgar Allan Poe was the first

Fig. 1. Lossing-Barritt, *Felix O. C. Darley.*
Wood engraving, ca. 1850 [Cat. No. 2]

The numerous lifetime portraits of Darley are one measure of the extent of his fame. This wood engraving by Lossing-Barritt, depicting a rather dashing young man, probably dates from Darley's early years in New York. Later portraits include a wood engraving by Samuel Putnam Avery, probably from the early 1860s, an etching by Henry Bryan Hall, and numerous photographs. A stereo photograph by the New York photographers E. and H. T. Anthony was extravagantly titled *Darley, Artist – The Inimitable* (see frontispiece).

Fig. 2. F.O.C. Darley, *The News-Boy*. Tinted lithograph for
In Town and About (Philadelphia, 1843) [Cat. No. 12]

American humor has always relied heavily on pictures. The stories in *In Town and About* were based on lithographs after Darley's drawings rather than the other way around. This lithograph inspired "The News-Boy," an account by Joseph C. Neal of a Philadelphia street urchin who is left behind when his family moves West. The urban underworld of Neal's humorous sketches contrasts with the backwoods setting of much contemporary American humor.

of many authors to recognize his potential, and two of Darley's drawings appeared as illustrations for Poe's short story "The Gold Bug," on its first publication in *The Dollar Magazine* in 1843. Many of Darley's early illustrations for cheap editions of the regional fiction that was widely popular at the time reveal a crude vitality often lacking in his later work. Realistic portraits of the idlers and vendors who frequented Philadelphia's bustling streets were captured in a series of lithographs for the periodical *In Town and About*; as republished separately, they hold their own with the best of Darley's later work.

At the same time, the ambitious young artist was engaged in two projects on a distinctly grander scale: *Scenes in Indian Life* and illustrations for Sylvester Judd's novel *Margaret*. In these large-format, full-page illustrations, Darley abandoned the rough and sketchy draughtsmanship of his earliest work and adopted a refined outline style clearly inspired by Flaxman and Retzsch. Both the Noble Savages in *Scenes in Indian Life* and the backwoods characters in Judd's *Margaret* are highly idealized and romanticized, a dramatic change from the rough street thugs in *In Town and About* (see fig. 2). This shift in focus was as sudden as it was dramatic: the designs for *Margaret* remained unpublished for more than ten years, but *Scenes in Indian Life* appeared in 1843, the very same year as *In Town and About*. Although Darley continued to do work for Philadelphia publishers throughout his life, in 1848 he moved to New York City, which would remain his home for the next eleven years. Here he was greeted as "an artist of great force and originality, with the strictest fidelity to truth and character" capable of designs "of superior elegance and luxury."[2] He was not yet thirty years old. Immediately he began forging the friendships with authors and publishers which would prove such a remarkable feature of his career.

Several sketches (see, for example, fig. 5) record Darley's visit to Sunnyside, Washington Irving's home in Tarrytown, in July 1848,[3] and Irving's *Sketch Book* and *Rip Van Winkle* were the first books that Darley illustrated upon his move to New York. Subsequently, Darley went on to illustrate all of Irving's major works, including *The Legend of Sleepy Hollow*, *The Alhambra*, *Tales of a Traveller*, *Wolfert's Roost* (fig. 6), Knickerbocker's *History of New York*, and a monumental five-volume *Life of Washington*. Irving was delighted with Darley's portrayals of his characters, in particular Diedrich Knickerbocker, who, Irving felt, should "carry the air of being profoundly impressed with the truth of his own history."[4] Darley's illustrations for both *Rip Van Winkle* and *The Legend of Sleepy Hollow* were published by the American Art-Union, which had been established in 1839 to promote the work of American artists and to encourage Americans to become art collectors and patrons; works depicting American subject matter were especially encouraged. An edition of *Rip Van Winkle* illustrated with six lithographs by Darley was one of the premiums offered to members in 1848. This ambitious undertaking – essentially an early American *livre d'artiste* – bears comparison with such European publications as the 1828 edition of Goethe's *Faust* illustrated by Eugène Delacroix. The *Bulletin* of the American Art-Union confidently predicted that "the publication of [*Rip Van Winkle*] will mark an era in American Art. . . . [Darley's illustrations] tell the story as significantly as Irving has done it in words."[5] The following year, the Art-Union issued Irving's *Legend of Sleepy Hollow*, with similar illustrations by Darley. These two works remained among Darley's most popular; they were republished as recently as 1974 with added coloring by the twentieth-century illustrator Fritz Kredel. Color printing was still in its infancy in the 1840s and the colored book illustrations of that day were either extremely crude or prohibitively expensive; consequently, only a very few of Darley's original illustrations were colored – and that coloring was generally added by hand, not printed.[6] Following Irving's death in 1859, Darley executed a commemorative portrait, depicting him seated in his library at Sunnyside surrounded by his fellow authors. The publication of a large-scale engraving of this portrait was promoted as a "national event," embodying the native genius for literature and art.

Although the outline style Darley used for *Rip Van Winkle* and *The Legend of Sleepy Hollow* was inspired by Flaxman and Retzsch, with Retzsch's illustrations for Goethe and Schiller providing par-

15

[text continues on page 20]

Fig. 3.

Fig. 4. After F.O.C. Darley, *Indian Hunting Buffalo*.
Steel-engraved banknote design, published
by Toppan, Carpenter & Co., 1853 [Cat. No. 116]

Darley's account book lists a payment of $60 from the banknote engravers Toppan, Carpenter, Casilear & Co. on October 26, 1853, for a design depicting "Indians hunting buffaloes." This was one of more than thirty designs that Darley produced for the firm during the latter part of that year.

Opposite: Fig. 3. F.O.C. Darley, *Indian Hunting Buffalo*.
Preliminary drawing in graphite for a banknote design,
ca. 1853 [Cat. No. 115]

In general, Darley idealized the American Indian, contributing to the popular nineteenth-century concept of the Noble Savage. *Indian Hunting Buffalo* is related to his early *Scenes in Indian Life* (1843), but was actually executed somewhat later, as a design for an 1853 banknote engraving (above).

Fig. 5. James D. Smillie after F.O.C. Darley,
Washington Irving. Etching, 1859 [Cat. No. 28]

This etching by James D. Smillie is based on a drawing of Washington Irving and his little dog
Ginger that Darley made at Sunnyside in July 1848, about the time that the artist first became
acquainted with the author. Smillie's etching was published in 1859, the year Irving died.

Opposite: Fig. 6. J. W. Orr after F.O.C. Darley.
Wood-engraved title page (proof with graphite notes by the artist and engraver)
for Washington Irving, *Wolfert's Roost*, 1855? [Cat. No. 36]

Wood engraving was the process most commonly used for book and magazine illustrations in the
nineteenth century, and many of Darley's illustrations, especially for works with a wide popular
distribution, were executed in this technique. This proof for the title page of Washington Irving's
Wolfert's Roost is especially interesting because it includes Darley's notes to the engraver, J. W. Orr.

ticularly important prototypes, Darley applied this style to specifically American subjects, beginning with Sylvester Judd's novel *Margaret*,[7] even before leaving Philadelphia. Forgotten today, *Margaret* was extravagantly admired in the nineteenth century. Nathaniel Hawthorne considered it one of the books most characteristic of American writing, and James Russell Lowell called it the most emphatically *American* book ever written and found in its roughness an expression of the nation's frontier spirit.[8] Set in the hills of western New England in the last part of the eighteenth century, *Margaret* is the story of a girl raised among rough backwoodsmen; after her brother Chilion is executed for murdering a boorish youth who makes advances to Margaret at a husking bee, Margaret at last finds solace in Christianity. Darley was no doubt attracted by vivid descriptions of local characters such as Tony Washington, the black fiddler (figs. 7, 8), the Widow Wright, the old herbalist, and Brown Moll, a hard-bitten farm wife who is Margaret's foster mother, and of characteristic settings, such as a camp meeting and the husking bee.

Although he temporarily abandoned work on *Margaret* on moving to New York to concentrate on his commissions from the American Art-Union, Darley began a new series of *Margaret* illustrations in about 1850. The project then went through several distinct stages before its final publication in 1856; a number of Darley's preliminary drawings and early proofs, reflecting changes made during the evolution of Darley's designs, are in the Print Collection of The New York Public Library. One significant change is that while Darley himself drew the earliest versions directly on the stones (see fig. 7), the published lithographs were executed by the reproductive printmaker Konrad Huber (see fig. 8). This probably reflects Darley's growing prestige as a draughtsman and the absence of a tradition of artist-printmakers in the United States as well as the growing demands on his time from numerous commissions and projects during this period. The idea that a major artist might choose to make prints as a form of original expression did not really gain acceptance on this side of the Atlantic until the etching revival at the end of the nineteenth century. Darley's use of an

outline style in these early illustrations finds an interesting parallel in the writings of James Fenimore Cooper. In his *Notions of the Americans* (1828), Cooper had noted that "Until now the Americans have been tracing the outline of their great national picture. The work of filling up has just seriously commenced."[9] Coincidentally, Darley developed his mature three-dimensional style with fully shaded figures and backgrounds in the steel engravings that he designed for Cooper's works.

Darley's earliest illustrations for works by Cooper were four lithographs published in the *Bulletin* of the American Art-Union in 1851, the year that Cooper died. Both compositionally and technically, these prints are less impressive than those illustrating *The Legend of Sleepy Hollow* and *Rip Van Winkle*, which the Art-Union had published in 1848 and 1849. Nevertheless, in 1856, shortly after the publication of *Margaret*, Darley received a commission from W. A. Townsend & Co. for illustrations for Cooper's complete works (figs. 9, 10). This was a tremendous undertaking, involving a total of sixty-four steel engravings and 120 wood engravings, and was advertised by the publisher as a "Monument of American Art."[10] The thirty-two volumes in the series were first published in 1859–61, and frequently reprinted. Darley's illustrations were also published separately, a sure measure of their success. In them, he first achieved the assured and polished style that would characterize all his later works, and he always considered them among his finest achievements. Steel engraving, with its capacity for rendering fine details with sharpness and precision, was much admired in the nineteenth century. It was considered superior to both lithography and wood engraving, which were looked down upon as cheap, commercial processes. One contemporary critic even charged cheap popular prints – such as the lithographs of Currier and Ives – with injuring steel engraving, "which is a far purer and more instructive branch of art."[11] Darley's close association with the steel engraving was recognized, and one contemporary critic characterized him as "the prophet of the new dispensation in steel-engraving."[12]

Although Darley is primarily known as the illustrator of the

New York authors Irving and Cooper, he also illustrated works by the great New England writers Henry Wadsworth Longfellow and Nathaniel Hawthorne. Darley became acquainted with Longfellow in the 1850s, and the poet was present at the artist's marriage to Jane Colburn in Cambridge, Massachusetts, in 1859. Later, Longfellow helped Darley obtain a photograph of Hawthorne for use in his picture *Washington Irving and His Literary Friends at Sunnyside*, in which both Longfellow and Hawthorne are featured.[13] Although Darley illustrated individual poems by Longfellow much earlier, his large outline illustrations for Longfellow's *Evangeline* (see, for example, fig. 17) and Hawthorne's *Scarlet Letter* date from the 1880s, the last decade of his career. Darley dedicated his illustrations of *The Scarlet Letter* "To Henry Wadsworth Longfellow in memory of a Friendship of many years." Many of Darley's books from the late 1850s onward, including his Longfellow and Hawthorne illustrations as well as numerous editions of the works of Charles Dickens, were published in Boston by Houghton Mifflin and Company.

Certain typical subjects recur in Darley's work throughout his career. These include depictions of Native Americans and pioneers, and scenes from American history, especially the Revolutionary War and the life of George Washington. As early as 1843, Darley showed an interest in portraying characteristic "types." Many of his illustrations for *In Town and About* belong to the tradition established in European books of trades and representations of itinerant street vendors crying their wares. Although Darley did not transcribe the cries of the tradesmen he depicted in his book, he did portray a wide array of types, including the butcher, the butcher's boy, the drayman, the huckster, the newsboy (see fig. 2), the organ grinder, and the wood sawyer, as well as horse traders and fishmongers in his pictures of the horse market and the fish market. Ten years later, in 1853, he provided the illustrations for John L.

Overleaf: Fig. 7. F.O.C. Darley, *Tony Washington* (1st version).
Lithograph for *Compositions in Outline. . .from Judd's Margaret*,
ca. 1850 [Cat. No. 41]

This version of *Tony Washington* is one of the last lithographs that Darley himself drew on the stone. The figure resembles the black musicians in contemporary paintings by the Long Island artist William Sidney Mount. Both this and the later version of the print (see fig. 8) are dignified depictions of the old fiddler. The earlier studies for *Judd's Margaret* tend to be smaller than the later ones, probably reflecting a change in the scale of the project at some point during its lengthy evolution.

Fig. 8. K. Huber after F.O.C. Darley, *Tony Washington* (2nd version).
Lithograph for *Compositions in Outline . . .from Judd's Margaret*
(New York: J. S. Redfield, 1856) [Cat. No. 42]

Konrad Huber's lithograph after Darley's design appeared in the book *Compositions in Outline . . .from Judd's Margaret* in 1856; it is not known why Darley decided not to make the lithographs for this publication. As far as is known, from this time on he made no more original prints, perhaps because he was so sought after as a draughtsman.

Fig. 7.

Drawn by F. O. C. Darley.   Sarony & Co. Imp.   E. Huler. Sc.

Tony Washington.

Fig. 8.

McConnel's *Western Characters*, a similar gallery of characteristic types associated with the settlement of the frontier, including the voyageur, the pioneer, the ranger, the regulator, the peddler, the politician, and the Indian. Similar types recur with great frequency in Darley's illustrations both for fiction and for historical works.

Most of Darley's Native Americans (see, for example, figs. 3, 4) conform to the two stereotypes of Indians that were current in the mid-nineteenth century: the noble child of nature and the blood-thirsty savage.[14] Positive and romanticized portrayals of Indians in *Scenes in Indian Life* (1843) and the novels of James Fenimore Cooper (see figs. 9, 10) are balanced by scenes of violence such as *The Massacre of Wyoming* and *Mrs. (Mary) Rowlandson and Her Captors*. Some of Darley's best illustrations, however, suggest a more sympathetic view. An illustration for Washington Irving's *Sketch Book* (1848) depicts the death of King Philip, whom Irving described as "a patriot attached to his native soil, a prince true to his subjects, a soldier daring in battle."[15] An illustration for John W. De Forest's *History of the Indians of Connecticut* (1851) depicts the Pequots' heroic last stand against overwhelming odds. The conflict between Native Americans and the settlers who displaced them continued throughout the nineteenth century, so images such as these were fraught with emotional content and political implications for the artists' contemporaries, and the sometimes disturbing ambivalence of Darley's Indian imagery is a reflection of attitudes that were widespread at the time.

Like his depictions of Native Americans, Darley's portrayals of pioneers and settlers are sharply polarized between the real and the ideal, with Cooper's backwoodsmen again representing the romantic extreme. More earthy and realistic characters appear in comic novels of the 1840s and 1850s such as John S. Robb's *Streaks of Squatter Life* and Joseph M. Field's *The Drama in Pokerville*.[16] The illustrations in McConnel's *Western Characters* were more straightforward, but with his talent for caricature, Darley was unable to resist exaggerating the dour, wizened features of the frontier schoolmistress and the pompous self-absorption of the western politician. The difficulties and frustrations of pioneer life were fur-

ther mocked in *A New Home: Who'll Follow?* by Caroline M. Kirkland, which Darley illustrated in 1850. In contrast, the heroic strain is dominant in Darley's illustrations for *Pioneers in the Settlement of America* (1876–77), a massive two-volume celebration of Manifest Destiny, as "civilization establishes itself on the Atlantic coast, subdues the forest, makes the wilderness bloom, and advances westward, over mountains and across plains, to the Pacific."[17] Published in Boston in the year of the nation's centennial, *Pioneers in the Settlement of America* was advertised as "a beautiful specimen of American art and workmanship."[18]

Streaks of Squatter Life, The Drama in Pokerville, Western Characters, A New Home: Who'll Follow? and *Pioneers in the Settlement of America* were all illustrated with wood engravings.[19] Wood engraving was the printmaking process most frequently used for book and magazine illustrations during the nineteenth century. The artist drew his design directly on the endgrain of a block of boxwood. Since boxwood is a relatively small shrub, the woodblocks obtained from it are not very big; large designs could be accommodated only by bolting several small pieces of boxwood together. The block was then carved by highly skilled – and highly specialized – wood engravers. Since wood engraving was a relief process like letterpress printing, the woodblocks could be combined with type on the same page and printed on the same presses at the same time. This was a distinct advantage over lithography and steel engraving, which required special presses and could not be as easily combined with text. Athough some critics complained of the crudity of wood-engraved designs, the most talented wood engravers were capable of work of great delicacy and refinement. Darley's notes on a proof of a wood engraving by J. W. Orr (see fig. 6) suggest that he worked just as closely with the wood engravers who executed his designs as he did with the steel engravers.

For nineteenth-century writers and artists in search of heroic themes from the American past, the Revolutionary War provided an especially rich source of patriotic incidents and images. Certain events, such as the Battles of Lexington and Concord, Washington crossing the Delaware, and the winter at Valley Forge, assumed an iconographic importance entirely unrelated to their actual historic significance and appear repeatedly in paintings, prints, and book illustrations. In their depictions of Lexington and Concord, artists often portrayed American farmers leaving their plows, like the classical hero Cincinnatus, to fight for their country. Images of Washington crossing the Delaware were probably influenced by French portraits of Napoleon crossing the Alps – which, in turn, reflect historical accounts of Hannibal crossing the Alps in antiquity. Darley's depiction of Washington visiting his sick and wounded troops at Valley Forge is probably based on Antoine Jean Gros's image of a Christ-like Napoleon visiting the plague-house in Jaffa. In each case, the American subject was closely linked to an earlier historical tradition.

Darley depicted many such subjects throughout his career, but he also favored less familiar scenes. His prints of *Nancy Hart* and of *Elisabeth Grace and Rachel Martin* (figs. 11, 12), depicting female heroines, are based on accounts in *The Women of the American Revolution* by Elizabeth Fries Ellet. The large tinted lithographs were executed and printed in France, and published by Goupil & Co. in 1853. The fact that the prints have captions in both French and English suggests that they were offered for sale in France as well as in the United States. Although Goupil & Co. opened its New York office in the mid-1840s, the firm did not begin commissioning pictures from American artists until 1852;[20] Darley's two prints are among the first American prints they published. The crispness and precision of the work of the French lithographers contrasts with the far cruder and simpler prints being produced by American firms at this time. Michel Knoedler continued to publish lithographs of Darley's designs after he bought out Goupil's interest in the New York firm in 1857; "Darley's American Farm Scenes," a series of four lithographs representing the Four Seasons, were published by Knoedler in 1860.

Revolutionary War scenes also figure prominently in Darley's illustrations for works of fiction, including *The Spy*, by James Fenimore Cooper, and William Gilmore Simms's sensational Revolutionary romances, and for serious historical works such as Francis

L. Hawks, David L. Swain, and William A. Graham's *Revolutionary History of North Carolina* (1853). On this project, Darley collaborated with Benson John Lossing, who was himself an artist as well as a wood engraver and the prolific author of numerous historical works. Darley contributed the book's lively frontispiece and Lossing supplied the more mundane views of battlefields and other historic sites. Darley and Lossing collaborated again on *Our Country: A Household History of the United State*s (1876–77), for which Lossing wrote the text and for which Darley provided more than 500 designs, ranging from small vignettes to full-page illustrations.

The nineteenth century saw the creation of a virtual cult of George Washington as the country's greatest hero.[21] Darley's most important contribution to Washington iconography was his illustrations for Washington Irving's five-volume *Life of George Washington*. An early series of designs, commissioned by the publisher George P. Putnam in 1853, depicted scenes from Washington's childhood, such as *Washington and His Father in the Garden* and *Washington as Peacemaker*, the latter showing a very young Washington intervening in a scuffle between his schoolmates. The prototypes for such scenes were probably Horace Vernet's illustrations of the life of Napoleon, which included similar youthful episodes. Such apocryphal incidents were not deemed suitable for Putnam's 1857–59 publication of Irving's *Life of Washington*, in which reproductions of historic portraits, views, and maps formed the bulk of the illustrations, enlivened by twelve steel engravings after Darley, depicting a more mature and dignified hero. Their subjects include Washington and Fairfax fox-hunting; Washington responding to the appeal of the people of Winchester, Virginia, for protection from an Indian attack; and Washington subduing a camp brawl, as well as more common subjects such as Washington crossing the Delaware and Washington at Valley Forge. The illustration of Washington subduing a camp brawl is essentially an updated version of the earlier *Washington as Peacemaker*. George Washington is also the central figure in one of Darley's largest prints, *The Triumph of Patriotism* (1858), in which the return of the American troops to New York City following the departure of the British is

Fig. 9. James Smillie after F.O.C. Darley, *The Prisoners*.
Steel engraving (working proof) for *Pages and Pictures from the Writings of James Fenimore Cooper* (New York: W. A. Townsend & Co., 1861) [Cat. No. 53]

Darley was a draughtsman, not a printmaker; throughout his career, his drawings were almost always reproduced by other men as wood engravings, steel engravings, or lithographs. This early proof, depicting a scene from James Fenimore Cooper's *The Last of the Mohicans*, was pulled before the plate was completely engraved and shows the engraver's working methods (see the final version in fig. 10, opposite). It is part of a large group of progressive proofs given to the Library by the engraver's son, James D. Smillie.

Fig. 10. James Smillie after F.O.C. Darley, *The Prisoners*.
Steel engraving (final version, signed by artist and engraver) for
Pages and Pictures from the Writings of James Fenimore Cooper
(New York: W. A. Townsend & Co., 1861) [Cat. No. 55]

This final version of *The Prisoners* is the one that would have appeared in the published book. The fine detail that could be achieved in steel engravings was much admired in the nineteenth century. Because the process was more expensive than wood engraving or lithography, books illustrated with steel engravings were usually deluxe productions, aimed at a more exclusive audience.

equated with a Roman triumph, and in *Washington's Adieu to His Generals* (1860), an improbably grandiose depiction of Washington's departure from New York on the Whitehall Ferry. Both prints were inspired by Irving's *Life of Washington*, and *The Triumph of Patriotism* was dedicated to that author by its engraver and publisher, Alexander Hay Ritchie. It is likely that both *The Triumph of Patriotism* and *Washington's Adieu to His Generals* were attempts to rival Emmanuel Leutze's great painting, *Washington Crossing the Delaware*, a print of which had been published by Goupil & Co. in 1853. Although both Washington's entry into New York and his farewell to his generals were portrayed by other artists of the period, neither subject achieved the popularity of Washington crossing the Delaware, and consequently they are far less familiar today.

The outbreak of the Civil War in 1861 provided Darley with the opportunity to portray contemporary battles using the same conventions and compositions that he had developed for scenes from earlier American history. While other artists portrayed the endless marches and the soldiers' life in camp, Darley chose to concentrate on heroic stands and charges, the traditional stock in trade of battle painters since the seventeenth century. To modern viewers, whose vision of the Civil War has been shaped by the battlefield photographs of Mathew Brady and Alexander Gardiner, such grand presentations can appear unrealistically dramatic and dated. Contemporary viewers, however, were impressed with Darley's realism. Although subjects such as *The Charge of Young Dahlgren at Fredericksburg* were based on newspaper descriptions of the events, actual participants testified to "the accuracy with which the artist's imagination had caught and captured the local and personal facts."[22] Engravings after Darley's compositions began appearing as book illustrations as early as 1862 in Robert Tomes's *The War with the South* and in a novel by Ned Buntline (E.Z.C. Judson), *The Rattlesnake, or The Rebel Privateer*, and Darley contributed numerous illustrations of Civil War subjects to illustrated periodicals throughout the war. Civil War subjects also figured prominently in later histories such as Lossing's *Our Country*. The monumental engraving *On the March to the Sea* (fig. 13), depicting the Union general Sherman's campaign in Georgia, has sometimes been described as Darley's greatest work, and it is certainly one of the largest. Though some of his illustrations from this time suggest that Darley was not entirely without sympathy for the South – for example, a wood engraving entitled *Giving Comfort to the Enemy*, which shows a southern woman giving a drink of water to a thirsty Union soldier – *On the March to the Sea* appears to sanction and even glorify the havoc produced by the Union troops as they advanced, ripping up railroad ties, cutting telegraph wires, burning property – and freeing the slaves. Considering Darley's numerous depictions of George Washington, it seems surprising that he did not show an equal interest in Abraham Lincoln, who quickly became almost as great an American icon. Darley chose to concentrate instead on the Union military leaders, especially General George B. McClellan, of whom he executed at least two portraits. The first, based on a photograph by Mathew Brady, was published

Opposite: Fig. 11. F.O.C. Darley, *Elisabeth Grace and Rachel Martin*.
Preliminary drawings in graphite, black ink, and wash, ca. 1850 [Cat. No. 74]

These three lively studies for the lithograph reproduced as fig. 12 show Darley experimenting with the grouping of figures and horses. The general composition was probably inspired by a lithograph by the French Romantic painter Eugène Delacroix showing *Weislingen attacked by the men of Goetz* (1836). Echoes of compositions by Delacroix and other French Romantic artists such as Horace Vernet are to be found in Darley's work throughout his career.

N. Y. PUBLIC LIBRARY
PRINT DEPARTMENT.

in 1862, when McClellan was at the height of his success as commander of the Army of the Potomac. The second (fig. 16), an ambitious equestrian portrait, was reproduced as a bas-relief by the sculptor John Quincy Adams Ward in 1864, when McClellan was the democratic candidate for President, running against Lincoln. These heroic depictions of McClellan, and the absence of similar depictions of Lincoln, may well be a reflection of the artist's politics. A later design depicting *Grant as a Boy*, executed for the American Tract Society in 1869, is very much in the vein of Darley's earlier portraits of the young Washington. Other Civil War subjects by Darley appeared as banknote vignettes; The New York Public Library has a rough pencil sketch for one of these entitled *Freedom for the Slaves*. Some of these vignettes were used on the certificates issued by various states to veterans of the conflict.

Darley's designs appeared on numerous banknotes from the 1850s through the 1880s (see figs. 3, 4, 14, and the endpapers), a period that has been called the golden age of this miniaturist's art.[23] Examples appeared not only on paper money but also on bonds, stock certificates, and stamps. Skilled engravers were employed to create these tiny, extremely detailed compositions, which were all but impossible for forgers to duplicate. Typical subjects included scenes from American history – such as Darley's Civil War subjects – and rural and industrial labor, but one unusual design even depicted a visit from Saint Nicholas, inspired by the contemporary poem by Clement C. Moore. Although the engravings were tiny, Darley's original drawings were quite large in scale. Photography was used to reduce the designs to the required size and to transfer them to the plate for the engraver. James Smillie and Alfred Jones were among the engravers who carried out this painstaking work. A large collection of their engravings in The New York Public Library includes many of their banknote designs.

Photography could be used to transfer designs to woodblocks and steel plates for use as illustrations as well as for banknote vignettes. Previously, when the artist's final drawing had been made directly on the block, it had been destroyed in the process of engraving. The use of a photographic transfer process meant that the original drawing could be preserved, an increasingly important consideration because Darley's drawings were becoming highly appreciated and sought after in their own right. One of Darley's account books, which survives in a private collection, provides priceless documentation for the artist's work during the years 1853 to 1875; it records an increasing number of independent commissions for drawings and paintings that sold for increasingly higher prices as time went on.[24] These works were not intended for reproduction, though in some cases they were based on previous illustrations; they would have hung in the purchasers' homes and are another measure of Darley's increasing prestige as an artist. Photography could also be used to reproduce the artist's designs directly, without the intervention of an engraver or lithographer. As early as 1859, Darley experimented with *cliché-verre*, a process in which the artist drew directly on the treated glass plate, producing a negative from which his design could be printed photographically. In France, artists such as Corot and Daubigny created some significant works using the process, but Darley was one of a very few American artists to appreciate its merits.[25] By the 1860s, photographic reproductions of some of Darley's drawings were being offered for sale by New York photographers. Small *carte-de-visite* photographs of the four large wash drawings commissioned by the Prince Napoleon during a visit to New York (see figs. 14, 15) were issued by E. and H. T. Anthony in 1863 and photographs of some of Darley's Civil War subjects were sold by George Rockwood and John McClure.[26] In addition, many of the books published by Houghton Mifflin in the 1870s and 1880s were illustrated with photomechanical reproductions of Darley's drawings. Two lavish projects of this sort were *Compositions in Outline from Hawthorne's Scarlet Letter* (1879) and *Illustrations to Evangeline* (1882) (fig. 17). Although advertising copy by Houghton Mifflin praised the manner in which the reproductions conveyed the vigor and grace of the original drawings, in fact they are not as effective as earlier wood or steel engravings.[27] Photomechanical processes improved rapidly during the 1880s, however, and by the time Darley's last drawings, a series of characters from the works of Charles

Fig. 12. Claude Régnier after F.O.C. Darley, *Elisabeth Grace and Rachel Martin*. Tinted lithograph, published by Goupil & Co., New York, 1853 [Cat. No. 75]

Two of Darley's most dramatic compositions show the exploits of women during the struggle for American independence. *Elisabeth Grace and Rachel Martin* depicts two young women who disguised themselves as men in order to intercept British dispatches. These unusual subjects were based on accounts in Elizabeth Fries Ellet's *Women of the American Revolution*. Tinted lithographs such as this were probably the most accurate reproductions of Darley's designs. The middle tones provided by the tint stone faithfully capture the quality of the artist's original wash drawing.

Dickens (see, for example, fig. 18), were published by the Philadelphia firm Porter and Coates, they could be advertised without exaggeration as "magnificent illustrations carefully reproduced."[28] The proliferation of new and unfamiliar processes in this period must have been confusing as well as exciting, and not all publishers adopted the new technologies immediately. Magazine publishers in particular clung tenaciously to older methods. For some projects, Darley continued to execute his final drawings directly on the woodblock in the time-honored fashion at least as late as the 1870s.[29]

Following his marriage to Jane Colburn in 1859, the artist and his wife moved to Claymont, Delaware, to a large old house overlooking the Delaware River, where they lived with Darley's sisters Ellen and Julia and his brothers Edmund and Alfred. This lively and engaging family is still fondly remembered in their old neighborhood. Although according to some accounts Darley "withdrew from the cities"[30] at this time, it is clear that he maintained close relationships with his fellow artists, authors, and publishers both by letter and through frequent train trips to New York, Philadelphia, and Boston. His travels also took him considerably farther afield. He was an early visitor to the Adirondacks, and a wood engraving after one of his designs appeared in *Adventures in the Wilderness; or, Camplife in the Adirondacks* (1869), the book by William H. H. Murray that initiated tourism in that region. In 1872 he visited Mount Desert Island; two landscape drawings that he made in the vicinity of Bar Harbor were exhibited at the Century Club in 1874.[31] A visit to Canada is documented by additional drawings. It was also during these years that Darley and his wife visited Europe, where they spent thirteen months in 1866–67. Darley's account of their travels in England, France, Holland, Germany, and Italy was published in 1868 as *Sketches Abroad with Pen and Pencil* with illustrations after his own designs.

Darley remained at the height of his career in the 1870s. Many of his early works were being reissued and his name was constantly before the public. His designs continued to appear frequently in the illustrated periodicals that proliferated following the Civil War.

Illustration played a much larger role in such publications as *Harper's Weekly*, *The Aldine*, *Appleton's Journal*, and *Every Saturday* than it had in the much more modest journals of the 1840s and 1850s. To a large extent, the subjects Darley contributed are those for which he was already famous. Wood engravings after his designs of an *Indian Foray in the West* and *Farmers Nooning* appeared in *The Aldine* in 1870 and 1872, and *Street Musicians* and *The Newsboy* appeared in *The Illustrated Christian Weekly* in 1872 and 1873. His contributions to *Every Saturday* in the same period included *The Yankee Peddler*, *The Camp Meeting*, *The Quack Doctor*, and *The Drover*. Some of these subjects are direct reprises of early illustrations and reflect his ongoing interest in distinctly American incidents and characters. *The Newsboy* recalls his 1843 lithograph for *In Town and About* (fig. 2), and *The Camp Meeting* reflects his earlier treatment of the same theme in *Judd's Margaret* (1856). Two designs that appeared first in *Appleton's Journal* were later included in *Picturesque America*, which was issued by the same publisher in 1872–74. This ambitious project was advertised as "a monument of native art" and "the most magnificent illustrated work ever published in America," so it is not surprising that Darley was one of the "eminent American artists" selected for inclusion.[32] However, it is striking that both of Darley's contributions, *Emigrants Crossing the Plains* and *Californians Lassoing a Bear* appear to be at least twenty or thirty years out of date. Darley's heroic pioneers belong to the 1840s, the period so vividly described by Francis Parkman in *The California and Oregon Trail*, not to the 1870s, when most of the emigrants reached their destinations by railroad rather than ox-drawn covered wagons. Like many of Darley's later illustrations, these images reflect a nostalgic and romanticized view of the past. The editors at Appleton's recognized this disparity in date, commenting when Darley's design first appeared that "*The Emigrants Crossing the Plains* (so happily illustrated by the pencil of Darley . . .) of a few years ago are now the successful founders of cities and empires."[33]

Although Darley remained extremely popular, it is likely that by this period, both his subject matter and his style were beginning to appear somewhat out of date. This may not have hurt his reputation with the general public, whose tastes tend to be conservative, but it must have been apparent to more astute critics. Although Darley used photography as a tool, as a reproductive medium, and even – in his experiments with *cliché-verre* – as a medium of expression, photographs exerted no obvious stylistic influence on his work. While in the work of other illustrators this influence results in an increased sharpness of focus or in an increased informality of composition, there is no trace of such changes in Darley's designs. Similarly, there is no sign that Darley was aware of the many European artistic movements that began to influence American artists in the second half of the nineteenth century: the Pre-Raphaelites in England, the Realists and the Impressionists in France. Japanese influence appeared in American wood-engraved book illustration as early as 1865 in a striking design by John La Farge for Tennyson's *Enoch Arden*, published in Boston by Ticknor and Fields,[34] but Darley's contribution to the same book is in his usual style. Even toward the end of his career, Darley remained true to his beginnings. The chief influences, even on his late work, remained the art of the 1820s, 30s, and 40s, especially the great European Romantic artists such as Flaxman, Retzsch, Delacroix, and Vernet.

Although Darley was influenced by European artists throughout his career and had begun a series of Dickens illustrations as early as 1860, it was only toward the very end of his life that he deliberately set out to rival his European contemporaries. Dickens presented a special challenge, since so many of the greatest British artists had already illustrated his works. It is therefore especially significant that Darley's Dickens illustrations were admired in England, where they were considered "very refined both as regards conception and execution, and . . . especially interesting as indicating an intelligent appreciation on the part of a Transatlantic artist, of the novelist's characterisation, the extravagant and grotesque being instinctively avoided."[35] Darley was working on yet another series of Dickens illustrations at the time of his death in 1888. A drawing of *Dick Swiveller and Quilp* (fig. 18) was his last work, according to an inscription written on it by his wife, Jane. Other European subjects also play an increasingly larger role in his work during his last years. A series of illustrations for Thomas Percy's *Sir Gillum of Mydeltoun* and another for Elizabeth Barrett Browning's *The Rhyme of the Duchess May* were both left unfinished at his death.[36] Although the subjects of the drawings – especially those depicting the young couple in the Browning poem leading the knight's charger up the stairs to the battlements of the castle – strike the modern viewer as humorous rather than moving, Darley's compositional skills remain unimpaired and his draughtsmanship is as assured as in the best of his early drawings.

Darley's achievements were widely recognized at the time of his death, and his position as America's foremost illustrator seemed secure. In a talk delivered at the Grolier Club on the day after Darley's death, Lewis C. Fraser, the manager of the art department of *Century Magazine*, eulogized him as "the illustrator par excellence in America."[37] However, twelve years later, when an exhibition of his work was held at the Metropolitan Museum of Art, it was necessary to explain, in an almost apologetic tone, that Darley "confined himself almost entirely to outline drawing and black-and-white, and mainly to illustrations of publications." A new generation of illustrators had arisen, and the style of illustration at the turn of the century was radically different. Although in Darley's day, color printing was not economically feasible in the type of publications that he illustrated, by 1900 it was commonplace. The illustrations of Darley's successors – Edwin Austin Abbey, Howard and Katharine Pyle – and later N. C. Wyeth and Maxfield Parrish – were invariably photomechanically reproduced, usually in color. While Darley participated in the transition from traditional wood engraving, steel engraving, and lithography to photogravure, collotype, and photolithography, he did not live quite long enough to benefit from the development of color printing at the end of the nineteenth century. Although the artists of the next generation continued to explore many of the same themes that Darley had treated earlier in the century, they generally did so in color and in a strikingly different style. A new interest in the American past had

Fig. 13. A. H. Ritchie after F.O.C. Darley,
On the March to the Sea.
Proof before letters for the engraving published by
Stebbins, Hartford, Conn., 1868 [Cat. No. 88]

Sometimes described as Darley's greatest work, *On the March to the Sea* depicts the Union general Sherman's march through Georgia, leaving devastation in his wake. The engraving by A. H. Ritchie, measuring 32 by 40 inches (larger than many oil paintings) is a good example of the large-scale prints after Darley's designs which were sold during the 1850s and 1860s. Line engraving was the most highly esteemed reproductive process in the mid- to late nineteenth century, even though the engraver was obliged to use dense patterns of lines and hatching to interpret the shaded areas for which Darley generally used wash in his original drawings.

emerged in the context of the Colonial Revival, and artists sought to reinterpret historical subjects with greater realism and increased attention to authentic detail. If Darley's work was beginning to seem out of date in the 1870s, by 1900 it must have appeared hopelessly old-fashioned compared to the lively, colorful work of Abbey, Wyeth, and Pyle. The exhibition at the Metropolitan Museum was an attempt to reassert Darley's importance in the light of these developments. He was hailed as "the most famous artist of the day in his own line," and his long list of achievements was reiterated:

> His name will always be associated with the works of Cooper, Irving, Judd, Hawthorne, Longfellow, Simms, and other American authors. . . . He also executed a number of large drawings relating to the history of the Revolution and the Civil War. Several important engravings were made from these and other compositions, such as *Wyoming, The First Blow for Liberty, Washington's Entry into New York, Foraging in Virginia, The Brave Charge of Young Dahlgren at Fredericksburg, Va.*, and *The Seasons*, representing various phases of American farm life.
>
> He also executed, for the private collection of the Prince Napoleon, four characteristic scenes – *Emigrants Attacked by Indians, The Village Blacksmith, The Unwilling Laborer, Repose*. Some of his most admirable works were made for the American Bank Note Co., mainly in vignette form, which comprised commercial, Indian and domestic incidents.[38]

Many of these works are represented in the present exhibition. The text concluded by quoting from the biography of Darley that had appeared in Henry Tuckerman's *Book of American Artists* (1870): "We have nothing . . . to compare with the exquisite and impressive drawings in which Darley has embodied his sense of . . . beauty, power and truth." Ironically, it was in part this very tendency of Darley's to idealize his subject matter that caused his drawings to appear somewhat dated in 1900, in comparison with the work of contemporary artists. A hundred years later, it is possible to look at Darley's work with greater objectivity and to recognize his real talent as a draughtsman, his importance as the first American illustrator to achieve an international reputation, and his pioneering role as the most important early illustrator of American fiction and history, the artist who probably did the most to help Americans of the mid-nineteenth century to visualize themselves and their past. For more than forty years, Darley dominated American book and magazine illustration. His illustrations were produced in large numbers for the mass market. They reached a tremendous audience in the nineteenth century and survive in substantial numbers today. They are still very accessible and they still have a great deal to teach us. In them, we can see Washington Irving's characters as Irving himself imagined them; we can see George Washington as he appeared to the Victorians, at once human and compassionate and heroic and larger-than-life; we can monitor changing attitudes toward the frontier and contemporary reactions to the Civil War. The greatest value of Darley's illustrations today is precisely that they do belong so very much to their own time. Taken as a whole, they provide a vivid contemporary panorama of nineteenth-century America recorded by an artist of genius. They are, as Victorian writers liked to say, "a monument of American art."

Fig. 14. F.O.C. Darley, *The Village Blacksmith*.
Drawing in black ink and wash, heightened with white, ca. 1863 [Cat. No. 104]

The Village Blacksmith, inspired by the Henry Wadsworth Longfellow poem of the same name, was one of four subjects executed by Darley for the Prince Napoleon, who visited the United States in 1861. This drawing is probably a copy of the one made for the Prince, for which Darley was paid $1,000. *The Village Blacksmith* was reproduced – much reduced – as a banknote design by the American Bank Note Company and as a photograph (see fig. 15, opposite).

Fig. 15. E. and H. T. Anthony after F.O.C. Darley,
The Village Blacksmith. Photograph, ca. 1863 [Cat. No. 114]

In the course of his long career, Darley explored a wide range of different media for reproducing his drawings, including lithography, wood engraving, and steel engraving, most of which required that a professional printmaker copy Darley's design. Photography was of special interest, because the photograph captured the appearance of the original drawing itself. Beginning in the 1860s, a number of Darley's works were published in the form of photographs.

Notes

1. At least, 1821 is the date that appears on Darley's tombstone in Mount Auburn Cemetery in Cambridge, Mass., according to information provided by Ray and Judith Hester. The best comprehensive study of Darley's life and work is still "... *Illustrated by Darley": An Exhibition of Original Drawings by the American Book Illustrator Felix Octavius Carr Darley* (Wilmington: Delaware Art Museum, 1978). Other useful references are listed in the bibliography of the present catalogue; see pp. 51–52.

2. *Bulletin of the American Art-Union*, no. 15 (November 25, 1848): 43–44.

3. Two such drawings are in the collections of Historic Hudson Valley. One, of Washington Irving and his little dog, is dated July 1848; the other, of "Sunnyside, Washington Irving's House on the Hudson," is dated July 24, 1848. Both drawings are reproduced in *Visions of Washington Irving: Selected Works from the Collections of Historic Hudson Valley* ([Tarrytown, N.Y.]: Historic Hudson Valley, [1991]), Nos. 48 and 49. Although these are authentic works by Darley, the watercolor drawings (No. 38) for *Rip Van Winkle* are not originals by him; they appear to be related to the 1974 publication by Historic Hudson Valley (then known as Sleepy Hollow Restorations) and are probably by Fritz Kredel.

4. Pierre M. Irving, *The Life and Letters of Washington Irving*, vol. 4 (New York: G. P. Putnam, 1864), p. 243. Quoted in Ethel King, *Darley, The Most Popular Illustrator of His Time* (Brooklyn, N.Y.: Theo Gaus' Sons, [1964]), p. 7.

5. *Bulletin of the American Art-Union*, no. 15 (November 25, 1848): 16–17.

6. Hand-colored examples of "Grandfather Lovechild's Nursery Stories" with illustrations by Darley are in the Sinclair Hamilton Collection at Princeton. A hand-colored impression of one of Darley's "American Farm Scenes" is in the Yale Unversity Art Gallery.

7. For a detailed study of Darley's illustrations for *Margaret*, see Sue W. Reed, "F.O.C. Darley's Outline Illustrations," *The American Illustrated Book in the Nineteenth Century*, ed. Gerald W. R. Ward (Winterthur, Del.: Henry Francis Du Pont Winterthur Museum, [1982]).

8. For a discussion of the contemporary reception of Judd's *Margaret*, see Richard D. Hathaway, *Sylvester Judd's New England* (University Park and London: Pennsylvania State University Press, [1981]), pp. 13f.

9. [James Fenimore Cooper], *Notions of the Americans Picked Up by a Travelling Bachelor*, vol. 2 (Philadelphia: Lea & Blanchard, 1843), p. 83. Cooper is actually speaking of population growth in the United States, but his metaphor is taken directly from the visual arts. *Notions of the Americans* was first published in 1828.

10. Publisher's Preface to *The Cooper Vignettes from Drawings by F.O.C. Darley* (New York: James G. Gregory, 1862), p. 6.

11. *Appleton's Journal*, February 6, 1869, p. 28.

12. "Book Illustrating in America," *Publisher's Weekly*, no. 851 (May 18, 1888): 779. The article is reporting on a talk given by Lewis C. Fraser, manager of the art department of *Century Magazine*, at the Grolier Club.

13. F.O.C. Darley, autograph letter signed to H[enry] W[adsworth] Longfellow, Claymont, Del., November 8, 1860; The Houghton Library, Harvard University. This letter includes Darley's request for a photograph of Hawthorne to be used in his picture. Other letters in the Houghton Library suggest a close relationship between Darley and Longfellow.

14. A discussion of the many inaccuracies in Darley's Indian designs may be found in John C. Ewers, "Not Quite Redmen: The Plains Indian Illustrations of Felix O. C. Darley," *The American Art Journal*, 3 (Fall 1971): 88–98.

15. [Washington Irving], *The Sketch Book* (New York: George P. Putnam, 1848), p. 382. Darley's depiction of the death of King Philip appears on the facing page.

16. See Georgia B. Barnhill, "F.O.C. Darley's Illustrations for Southern Humor," *Graphic Arts and the South*, ed. Judy L. Larson (Fayetteville: University of Arkansas Press, 1993), pp. 31–63. Darley's relations with some of these authors are also discussed in Paul Somers, Jr., *Johnson J. Hooper* (Boston: Twayne Publishers, [1984]) and in the introduction to Thomas Bangs Thorpe, *A New Collection of Thomas Bangs Thorpe's Sketches of the Old Southwest*, ed. David C. Estes (Baton Rouge and London: Louisiana State University Press, [1989]).

17. Quoted from the publisher's advertisement printed on the back of the original wrappers of William A. Crafts, *Pioneers in the Settlement of America* (Boston: Samuel Walker and Company, 1876–77).

18. Ibid.

19. Princeton University Library, *Early American Book Illustrators and Wood Engravers, 1670–1870*, 2 vols. (Princeton, N.J.: Princeton University Press, 1958–68) is still one of the best discussions of this technique and includes a good bibliography of books illustrated by Darley.

20. M. Knoedler & Company, *A Catalogue of an Exhibition of Paintings and Prints of Every Description on the Occasion of Knoedler, One Hundred Years, 1846–1946* (New York: M. Knoedler & Company, 1946), n.p.

21. Barbara J. Mitnick, *The Changing Image of George Washington* (New York: Fraunces Tavern Museum, 1989) is a useful discussion of this subject; however, Mitnick's Cat. No. 25 (Fig. 7), *The Triumph of Patriotism*, which is identified as a chromolithograph by Christian Inger after a design by Darley, is unrelated to Darley's version (No. 77 in the current exhibition and catalogue).

22. *Biographical Sketches of Benson J. Lossing, L.L.D., Author, and Felix O. C. Darley, Artist of Our Country, A Household History for All Readers* (New York: Johnson & Miles, [1876]), pp. 11–12.

23. See William H. Griffiths, *The Story of the American Bank Note Company* (New York: American Bank Note Company, 1959).

24. Darley's account book for 1853–75 is in the private collection of Elizabeth, Allen, and Martha Schiek. It is not always easy to distinguish between commissions for drawings intended for reproduction and those meant for personal use as art objects, but by the 1860s what appear to be private commissions appear in the account book with some frequency. In 1864, Henry F. Durant paid $500 for *Emigrants Surprised by Indians*; in 1869, Henry Howe paid $185 for "one design in color," *Saying Grace*; Mr.

Whitmore paid $200 for a "design in color," *Children on the Sea Shore*; and Charles Knickerbocker paid $495 for the "large watercolor" *Evening Prayer*, $350 for *Husking*, and $350 for *Visit to the Homestead*. A later note by Darley records that *Visit to the Homestead* was lost in the great fire in Chicago. Similar commissions continue to be recorded through the 1870s.

25. On the process, see Elizabeth Glassman and Marilyn F. Symmes, *Cliché-verre: Hand-Drawn, Light Printed* (Detroit: Detroit Institute of Arts, 1980). Darley's contribution to John W. Ehninger's *Autograph Etchings by American Artists* is discussed on pp. 80–90 and reproduced on p. 192.

26. Anthony's photographs of the drawings for the Prince Napoleon are in the Print Collection, The New York Public Library. Anthony also sold portrait photographs of Darley, including the stereograph *Darley, Artist – The Inimitable*. Darley's account book (see note 24 above) lists arrangements with Rockwood "for permission to copy in photograph drawing The Story of a Battle, remitting 7 cts. per copy," and with McClure for "sales of photographs" of *Foraging Party* and *Cavalry Charge* paying "50 cents on each copy sold." Presumably the latter photographs were much larger in format.

27. *Publisher's Weekly*, no. 561 (October 14, 1882): 522. In announcing the publication of *Darley's Illustrations to Evangeline* for October 21, Houghton Mifflin and Company assured readers that "The designs have been reproduced in a manner which brings out effectively their vigor and grace; they have been printed on a hand press to assure the best possible result."

28. "Christmas Bookshelf," special number of *Publisher's Weekly*, (1888): 2.

29. The account book (see note 24) lists "2 designs on wood" for The American Tract Society as late as February 19, 1873. The Print Collection includes a drawing on tracing paper for *Winter*, which was reproduced as a wood engraving in *The Illustrated Christian Weekly* on February 17, 1872.

Presumably this tracing was used to transfer Darley's design to the woodblock in order to preserve the original drawing.

30. For example, according to Frederic G. Kitton, in *Dickens and His Illustrators* (London: George Redway, 1899), p. 224: "[Darley] withdrew in his latter years from the cities to his home in Clayton [sic], Delaware, where he died, March 27, 1888." Kitton was drawing on information supplied by Houghton Mifflin and Company.

31. The two drawings exhibited at the Century Club were *Ovens, Mount Desert* and *Porcupine Islands, Mount Desert*. A third drawing, *Rocks Near the Landing at Bald Porcupine Island, Bar Harbor*, is reproduced in John Wilmerding, *The Artist's Mount Desert: American Artists on the Maine Coast* (Princeton, N.J.: Princeton University Press, [1994]), p. 138.

32. See Sue Rainey, *Creating Picturesque America: Monument to the Natural and Cultural Landscape* (Nashville and London: Vanderbilt University Press, 1994). Darley's illustrations are discussed on p. 205.

33. *Appleton's Journal of Literature, Science and Art*, I (1869): 601.

34. Princeton University Library, *Early American Book Illustrators and Wood Engravers, 1670–1870*, vol. I (Princeton, N.J.: Princeton University Press, 1958), p. 165 and fig. 89.

35. Ibid., p. 223.

36. Drawings for both projects are in the Print Collection of The New York Public Library.

37. Quoted in "Book Illustrating in America," *Publisher's Weekly*, no. 851 (May 19, 1888): 779.

38. What appears to be a poster or introductory panel for this exhibition is preserved in the private collection of Elizabeth, Allen, and Martha Schiek. The material in the 1900 exhibition was lent by Mrs. F.O.C. Darley, Mrs. William T. Blodgett, The American Bank Note Company, and Mr. Alfred Jones. Some of this material is now in The New York Public Library.

Checklist of the Exhibition

This exhibition represents but a small selection from the Darley material in the collections of The New York Public Library. The majority of the additional drawings, prints, and books illustrated by Darley are housed in the Print Collection of the Miriam and Ira D. Wallach Division of Art, Prints and Photographs. The core of the Print Collection's extensive holdings came from the Everett Augustus Duyckinck Collection, which was given to the Lenox Library in 1878. Additional material came from the art dealer Samuel Putnam Avery, who early in his career engraved some of Darley's designs on wood; from James David Smillie, whose father engraved many of Darley's works on copper and on steel; and from the artist's widow, Jane G. Darley, who gave two large groups of prints and drawings early in the twentieth century. A recent group of significant drawings was the gift of Carl H. Pforzheimer III. Additional books illustrated by Darley are to be found in the Library's Henry W. and Albert A. Berg Collection of English and American Literature, General Research Division, Manuscripts and Archives Division, and Rare Books Division.

This checklist includes entries for separate drawings and prints as well as for illustrated books and other related objects. Entries for individual prints and drawings begin with the names of the printmaker (where applicable) and artist. Books are listed under the name of the author. Unless otherwise noted, material is from the Print Collection. The order of the checklist reflects the arrangement of the exhibition at The New York Public Library.

1

B. Lander

F.O.C. Darley

Drawing in graphite, ca. 1850

Henry W. and Albert A. Berg Collection of English and American Literature

2

Lossing-Barritt (after B. Lander?)

Felix O. C. Darley

Wood engraving, ca. 1850

(fig. 1)

3

F.O.C. Darley

In Town and About (Philadelphia, 1843)

Illustrated with lithographs

4

F.O.C. Darley

The Fish Market

Tinted lithograph for *In Town and About*

(Philadelphia, 1843)

5

Johnson Jones Hooper

Adventures of Captain Simon Suggs

(Philadelphia: T. B. Peterson and Brothers, 1846)

Illustrated with wood engravings after F.O.C. Darley; with lithographed wrappers

General Research Division

6

Joseph C. Neal

The Misfortunes of Peter Faber and Other Sketches (Philadelphia: T. B. Peterson and Brothers, 1856)

Illustrated with wood engravings after F.O.C. Darley; with lithographed wrappers

7

F.O.C. Darley

"Sir, said he, . . . you have no objection to prayers?"

Drawing in graphite, black ink, and wash, ca. 1843, for Joseph M. Field, *The Drama in Pokerville, The Bench and Bar of Jurytown, and Other Stories* (Philadelphia, 1843 and later editions)

8

Gilbert & Gihon after F.O.C. Darley

"Sir, said he, . . . you have no objection to prayers?"

Wood engraving for Joseph M. Field, *The Drama in Pokerville, The Bench and Bar of Jurytown, and Other Stories* (Philadelphia, 1843 and later editions)

9

William Tappan Thompson

Major Jones's Courtship and Travels (Philadelphia: T. B. Peterson and Brothers, [1848])

Illustrated with wood engravings after Darley

General Research Division

10

F.O.C. Darley

Old Sugar, the Standing Candidate

Drawing in graphite and wash, ca. 1843, for John S. Robb, *Streaks of Squatter Life* (Philadelphia, 1843 and later editions)

11

F.O.C. Darley

Tinted lithograph (title page) for *In Town and About* (Philadelphia, 1843)

12

F.O.C. Darley

The News-Boy

Tinted lithograph for *In Town and About* (Philadelphia, 1843)

(fig. 2)

13

F.O.C. Darley

The Boys That Run with the Engine

Tinted lithograph for *In Town and About* (Philadelphia, 1843)

14

Hinckley after F.O.C. Darley

Wood-engraved cover for *The John-Donkey*, ca. 1848

15

F.O.C. Darley

Drawing in graphite for the cover design of *The Lantern*, ca. 1852

16

F.O.C. Darley

Drawing in graphite, black ink, and wash for an illustration for E. A. Poe, "The Gold Bug," 1843

17

F.O.C. Darley

Drawing in graphite and wash for the cover of *The American Art-Union Journal*, 1851

18
AFTER F.O.C. DARLEY
Wood-engraved cover for *The American Art-Union Journal*, 1851?

19
THOMAS OLDHAM BARLOW AFTER F.O.C. DARLEY AND CHRISTIAN SCHUSSELE
Washington Irving and His Literary Friends at Sunnyside
Engraving, published by the Irving Publishing Co., 1864

20
F.O.C. DARLEY
Illustrations of Rip Van Winkle (New York: The American Art-Union, 1848)
Illustrated with lithographs

21
F.O.C. DARLEY
Illustrations of The Legend of Sleepy Hollow (New York: The American Art-Union, 1849)
Illustrated with lithographs

22
WASHINGTON IRVING
Rip Van Winkle (London: Joseph Cundall, 1850)
Illustrated with hand-colored etchings by Charles Simms based on daguerreotypes of Darley's designs
Stuart Collection, Rare Books Division

23
WASHINGTON IRVING
Rip Van Winkle & The Legend of Sleepy Hollow ([Tarrytown, N.Y.]: Sleepy Hollow Restorations, [1974])

Illustrated with offset lithographs of designs by Darley, redrawn and colored by Fritz Kredel
Henry W. and Albert A. Berg Collection of English and American Literature

24
F.O.C. DARLEY
Rip Van Winkle and His Children
Lithograph for his *Illustrations of Rip Van Winkle* (New York: The American Art-Union, 1848)

25
F.O.C. DARLEY
The Return of Rip Van Winkle
Lithograph for his *Illustrations of Rip Van Winkle* (New York: The American Art-Union, 1848)

26
F.O.C. DARLEY
Ichabod Crane Dancing with Katrina Van Tassel
Lithograph (trial proof) for his *Illustrations of The Legend of Sleepy Hollow* (New York: The American Art-Union, 1849)

27
F.O.C. DARLEY
Ichabod Crane Dancing with Katrina Van Tassel
Lithograph for his *Illustrations of The Legend of Sleepy Hollow* (New York: The American Art-Union, 1849)

28
JAMES D. SMILLIE AFTER F.O.C. DARLEY
Washington Irving
Etching, 1859
(fig. 5)

29
F.O.C. DARLEY
Sunnyside, Residence of Washington Irving
Drawing in graphite, black ink, and wash for the title page of [Washington Irving], *The Sketch Book of Geoffrey Crayon, Gentn.* (New York: G. P. Putnam, 1848)

30
[WASHINGTON IRVING]
The Sketch Book of Geoffrey Crayon, Gentn. (New York: G. P. Putnam, 1848)
Illustrated with wood engravings after F.O.C. Darley

31
[WASHINGTON IRVING]
The Sketch Book of Geoffrey Crayon, Gentn. (New York: G. P. Putnam, 1848)
Illustrated with wood engravings after F.O.C. Darley; two original drawings tipped in
Inscribed "Julia A. Darley, from her brother F.O.C. Darley, Jany. 1st 1849." Signed by Washington Irving and Martha Washington
Manuscripts and Archives Division

32
F.O.C. DARLEY
The Angler
Drawing in brown ink and wash for [Washington Irving], *The Sketch Book of Geoffrey Crayon, Gentn.* (New York: G. P. Putnam, 1848)

33

F.O.C. Darley

Rip Van Winkle Awaking

Drawing in brown ink and wash for [Washington Irving], *The Sketch Book of Geoffrey Crayon, Gentn.* (New York: G. P. Putnam, 1848)

34

[Washington Irving]

A History of New York, from the beginning of the world to the end of the Dutch Dynasty . . . by Diedrich Knickerbocker (New York: G. P. Putnam, 1850)

Illustrated with wood engravings after F.O.C. Darley

35

Bobbett & Edmonds after F.O.C. Darley

William the Testy Astonishing the Council with His New Method of Waging War

Herrick after F.O.C. Darley

Van Poffenburg Practising War

Wood-engraved illustrations for [Washington Irving], *A History of New York, from the beginning of the world to the end of the Dutch Dynasty . . . by Diedrich Knickerbocker* (New York: G. P. Putnam, 1850)

36

J. W. Orr after F.O.C. Darley

Wood-engraved title page (proof with graphite notes by the artist and engraver) for Washington Irving, *Wolfert's Roost*, 1855?
(fig. 6)

37

The subscriber respectfully informs the public . . .

Wood-engraved and letterpress advertisement for J. W. Orr, Wood Engraver, ca. 1850

38

F.O.C. Darley

A Glimpse at the World

Preliminary drawing in brush and gray wash over graphite for *Compositions in Outline . . . from Judd's Margaret*, ca. 1846–47?

39

F.O.C. Darley

A Glimpse at the World (1st version)

Lithograph for *Compositions in Outline . . . from Judd's Margaret*, 1850

40

Compositions in Outline . . . from Judd's Margaret (New York: J. S. Redfield, 1856)

Illustrated with lithographs by K. Huber after F.O.C. Darley

41

F.O.C. Darley

Tony Washington (1st version)

Lithograph for *Compositions in Outline . . . from Judd's Margaret*, ca. 1850
(fig. 7)

42

K. Huber after F.O.C. Darley

Tony Washington (2nd version)

Lithograph for *Compositions in Outline . . . from Judd's Margaret* (New York: J. S. Redfield, 1856)
(fig. 8)

43

F.O.C. Darley

Camp Meeting

Drawing in graphite, ca. 1850?

44

K. Huber after F.O.C. Darley

Camp Meeting in the Woods

Lithograph for *Compositions in Outline . . . from Judd's Margaret* (New York: J. S. Redfield, 1856)

45

F.O.C. Darley

Three preliminary drawings in brush and gray wash over graphite for *Compositions in Outline . . . from Judd's Margaret*, ca. 1846–47

46

F.O.C. Darley

Brown Moll

Drawing in red wash, pen, brush, and black ink related to *Compositions in Outline . . . from Judd's Margaret*, ca. 1850

47

F.O.C. Darley

The Widow Wright (1st version)

Lithograph for *Compositions in Outline . . . from Judd's Margaret*, ca. 1850

48

K. Huber after F.O.C. Darley

The Widow Wright (2nd version)

Lithograph for *Compositions in Outline . . . from Judd's Margaret* (New York: J. S. Redfield, 1856)

49

K. Huber after F.O.C. Darley

The Husking Bee

Lithograph for *Compositions in Outline . . .
from Judd's Margaret* (New York: J. S.
Redfield, 1856)

50

K. Huber after F.O.C. Darley

The Murder

Lithograph for *Compositions in Outline . . .
from Judd's Margaret* (New York: J. S.
Redfield, 1856)

51

F.O.C. Darley

*Leather Stocking, Paul Hover and Ellen,
Concealing Themselves from the Indians*

Lithograph, published by The American Art-
Union, New York, 1851

52

F.O.C. Darley

*Leather Stocking at the Grave of Chingach-
gook*

Lithograph, published by The American Art-
Union, New York, 1851

53

James Smillie after F.O.C. Darley

The Prisoners

Steel engraving (working proof) for *Pages and
Pictures from the Writings of James Fenimore
Cooper* (New York: W. A. Townsend & Co.,
1861)

(fig. 9)

54

James Smillie after F.O.C. Darley

The Prisoners

Steel engraving (with artist's autograph notes
to the engraver) for *Pages and Pictures from
the Writings of James Fenimore Cooper* (New
York: W. A. Townsend & Co., 1861)

55

James Smillie after F.O.C. Darley

The Prisoners

Steel engraving (final version, signed by artist
and engraver) for *Pages and Pictures from the
Writings of James Fenimore Cooper* (New
York: W. A. Townsend & Co., 1861)

(fig. 10)

56

James Smillie after F.O.C. Darley

The Search

Steel engraving (with artist's autograph notes
to the engraver) for *Pages and Pictures from
the Writings of James Fenimore Cooper* (New
York: W. A. Townsend & Co., 1861)

57

John Whetton Ehninger

Autograph Etchings by American Artists (New
York: W. A. Townsend & Co., 1859)

Illustrated with *clichés-verre* by Darley and
others

58

The Cooper Vignettes (New York: J. G.
Gregory, 1862)

Illustrated with steel engravings and wood
engravings after F.O.C. Darley

59

F.O.C. Darley

*Hawthorne's Scarlet Letter with Illustrations
by F.O.C. Darley* (Boston: Houghton Mifflin
Co., 1884)

Illustrated with photomechanical reproductions of drawings

Fig. 16. F.O.C. Darley, *General George B. McClellan*.
Drawing in black ink and wash for a bas-relief, 1863 [Cat. No. 89]

This 1863 drawing by Darley served as the basis for a bas-relief of General George B. McClellan
by John Q. A. Ward. The bas-relief was issued the following year, when McClellan was the
Democratic candidate for the Presidency, running against Abraham Lincoln, who had dis-
missed him as commander of the Army of the Potomac in 1862. A contemporary advertisement
described the bas-relief as "a splendid contribution to American art . . . fit either for the Parlor,
Library, or Club Room."

60
F.O.C. Darley
"Then came the guard from the ships . . ."
Drawing in graphite for Henry Wadsworth
Longfellow, *Evangeline* (Boston and New
York: Houghton Mifflin and Company, 1883)
(fig. 17)

61
F.O.C. Darley
"Then came the guard from the ships . . ."
Photomechanical reproduction for Henry
Wadsworth Longfellow, *Evangeline* (Boston
and New York: Houghton Mifflin and
Company, 1883)

62
F.O.C. Darley
*Death of Gabriel: "Meekly she bowed her
[head] and murmured 'Father, I thank thee.'"*
Drawing in graphite for Henry Wadsworth
Longfellow, *Evangeline* (Boston and New
York: Houghton Mifflin and Company, 1883)

63
F.O.C. Darley
*Death of Gabriel: "Meekly she bowed her
[head] and murmured 'Father, I thank thee.'"*
Photomechanical reproduction for Henry
Wadsworth Longfellow, *Evangeline* (Boston
and New York: Houghton Mifflin and
Company, 1883)

64
J. G. McRae after F.O.C. Darley
[*The Massacre of Wyoming*]
Engraving (proof before letters), 1852

65
F.O.C. Darley
Scenes in Indian Life (Philadelphia: J. R.
Colon, [1843])
Illustrated with lithographs

66
F.O.C. Darley
Jacob Spaulding's Adventure
Drawing in graphite, black ink, and wash for
John W. De Forest, *History of the Indians of
Connecticut . . .* (Hartford: Wm. Jas.
Hamersley, 1851)

67
F.O.C. Darley
Death of King Philip
Drawing in graphite, brown ink, and wash for
[Washington Irving], *The Sketch Book of
Geoffrey Crayon, Gentn.* (New York: G. P.
Putnam, 1848)

68
F.O.C. Darley
[*Man on horseback*]
Preliminary drawing in graphite for the title
page of Francis Parkman, Jr., *The California
and Oregon Trail* (New York: George P.
Putnam, 1849)

69
Francis Parkman, Jr.
The California and Oregon Trail (New York:
George P. Putnam, 1849)
Illustrated with wood engravings after F.O.C.
Darley
General Research Division

70
Whitney-Jocelyn-Annin after
F.O.C. Darley
The Missionary and *The Pioneer*
Wood engravings for John Ludlum McConnel,
Western Characters (New York: Redfield,
1853)

71
H. B. Hall, Jr. after F.O.C. Darley
Emigrants Crossing the Plains
Steel engraving for *Picturesque America* (New
York: Appleton and Company, 1874)

72
F.O.C. Darley
Attack on a Wagon Train
Preliminary drawing in graphite for William
A. Crafts, *Pioneers in the Settlement of
America* (Boston: S. Walker and Co., 1876)

73
A. H. Ritchie after F.O.C. Darley
First Blow for Liberty
Engraving, published by Mason Brothers, New
York, 1858

74
F.O.C. Darley
Elisabeth Grace and Rachel Martin
Three preliminary drawings in graphite, black
ink, and wash, ca. 1850, for the lithograph
(fig. 11)

75
Claude Régnier after F.O.C. Darley
Elisabeth Grace and Rachel Martin
Tinted lithograph, published by Goupil & Co.,
New York, 1853
(fig. 12)

76
CLAUDE RÉGNIER AFTER F.O.C. DARLEY
Nancy Hart
Tinted lithograph, published by Goupil & Co.,
New York, 1853

77
A. H. RITCHIE AFTER F.O.C. DARLEY
*Triumph of Patriotism: Washington Entering
New York, 25th Nov. 1783*
Engraving, published by Ritchie & Co., New
York, 1858

78
F.O.C. DARLEY
*Washington Taking Leave of His Army at
Whitehall, N.Y.*
Preliminary drawing in graphite, 1852–53, for
the wood engraving

79
AFTER F.O.C. DARLEY
*Washington Taking Leave of His Army at
Whitehall, N.Y.*
Wood engraving for *The Illustrated New York
News* (February 1853)

80
AUGUSTUS KOELLNER AFTER F.O.C. DARLEY
The Women of '76: Tidings from Lexington
Lithograph for *Godey's Magazine*, early 1840s

81
Yankee Doodle (New York: Trent, Filmer &
Co., [1865])
Illustrated with wood engravings after F.O.C.
Darley; with lithographed wrappers

82
WHITNEY-JOCELYN-ANNIN AFTER
F.O.C. DARLEY
Wood-engraved title page for William Gilmore
Simms, *The Partisan* (New York: Redfield,
1854)

83
WHITNEY-JOCELYN-ANNIN AFTER
F.O.C. DARLEY
Wood-engraved title page for William Gilmore
Simms, *Katharine Walton* (New York:
Redfield, 1854)

84
WHITNEY-JOCELYN-ANNIN AFTER
F.O.C. DARLEY
Washington and His Father in the Garden
Washington as Peacemaker
Washington's Surveying Expedition
The Surveyor's Camp
Wood engravings for G. P. Putnam & Co.,
ca. 1853

85
WASHINGTON IRVING
The Life of George Washington (New York:
G. P. Putnam & Co., 1857–59)
Illustrated with steel engravings and wood
engravings after F.O.C. Darley and others
Rare Books Division

86
FRANCIS L. HAWKS, DAVID L. SWAIN, AND
WILLIAM A. GRAHAM
Revolutionary History of North Carolina
(Raleigh: William D. Cooke; New York:
George P. Putnam & Co., 1853)

Illustrated with wood engravings by Whitney-
Jocelyn-Annin after F.O.C. Darley
Stuart Collection, Rare Books Division

87
G. R. HALL AFTER F.O.C. DARLEY
*The People of Winchester Appealing to
Washington*

G. R. HALL AFTER F.O.C. DARLEY
Washington Subduing a Camp Brawl

DUTHIE AFTER F.O.C. DARLEY
Washington Crossing the Delaware

J. McGOFFIN AFTER F.O.C. DARLEY
Washington at Valley Forge

Steel engravings for Washington Irving, *Life of
George Washington* (New York: G. P. Putnam
& Co., 1857–59)

88
A. H. RITCHIE AFTER F.O.C. DARLEY
On the March to the Sea
Proof before letters for the engraving pub-
lished by Stebbins, Hartford, Conn., 1868
(fig. 13)

89
F.O.C. DARLEY
General George B. McClellan
Drawing in black ink and wash for the bas-
relief, 1863
(fig. 16)

90
JOHN Q. A. WARD AFTER F.O.C. DARLEY
General George B. McClellan
Bas-relief in bronze and silver, 1864

91
[Francis Scott Key]
The Star Spangled Banner (New York: J. G. Gregory, 1861)
Illustrated with wood engravings after F.O.C. Darley; with lithographed wrappers

92
A Selection of War Lyrics (New York: J. G. Gregory, 1864)
Illustrated with wood engravings after F.O.C. Darley

93
Richard Dudensing after F.O.C. Darley
Battle near Mill Springs
Steel engraving for Robert Tomes, *The War with the South* (New York and London: Virtue & Yorston, [1862–67])

94
W. Ridgeway after F.O.C. Darley
Battle of Shiloh, Tenn. – Charge of General Grant
Steel engraving for Robert Tomes, *The War with the South* (New York and London: Virtue & Yorston, [1862–67])

95
Brightly after F.O.C. Darley
The Escape from Libby
Wood engraving from an illustrated periodical, March 26, 1864

96
After F.O.C. Darley
George B. McClellan
Steel engraving, 1862

97
John H. Williams, Jr.
Advertisement for equestrian bas-relief of McClellan, September 15, 1864

98
Honor to Our Country's Brave Defenders
Engraved certificate (Resolution of Thanks presented to soldiers and sailors from New Jersey by the Legislature of New Jersey), July 4, 1866
Illustrated with steel engravings after Darley and others

99
Samuel Putnam Avery
F.O.C. Darley
Wood engraving, ca. 1862

100
E. and H. T. Anthony
Darley, Artist – The Inimitable
Stereo photograph, ca. 1862?
Photography Collection, Miriam and Ira D. Wallach Division of Art, Prints and Photographs
(frontispiece)

101
Bogert after F. B. Schnell
Home of F.O.C. Darley
Wood engraving, after 1859

102
Adolph Lafosse after F.O.C. Darley
Winter
Tinted lithograph, printed by Lemercier, Paris; published by M. Knoedler, New York, 1860

103
Charles Jérémie Fuhr after F.O.C. Darley
Summer
Tinted lithograph, printed by Lemercier, Paris; published by M. Knoedler, New York, 1860

104
F.O.C. Darley
The Village Blacksmith
Drawing in black ink and wash, heightened with white, ca. 1863
(fig. 14)

105
F.O.C. Darley
A Visit from Saint Nicholas
Preliminary drawing in graphite for a banknote design, ca. 1862

106
After F.O.C. Darley
A Visit from Saint Nicholas
Steel-engraved banknote design, ca. 1862

107
[Clement C. Moore]
A Visit from Saint Nicholas (New York: Hurd & Houghton, 1862)
Illustrated with wood engravings after F.O.C. Darley; with lithographed wrappers

108
F.O.C. Darley
Cattle and Herdboy
Preliminary drawing in black ink and wash, heightened with white, for a banknote design, 1859

Fig. 17. F.O.C. Darley, *"Then came the guard from the ships . . ."*
Drawing in graphite for Henry Wadsworth Longfellow, *Evangeline* (Boston and
New York: Houghton Mifflin and Company, 1883) [Cat. No. 60]

This vigorous sketch was a preliminary design for an 1883 edition of Longfellow's *Evangeline*.
Even at this late date, Darley used a rough expressionistic style for his early studies, which in this
case helps to emphasize the violent action of the scene. The final drawing, which was much
smoother and more polished, was reproduced using an early photomechanical process that was
not very effective, and the resulting illustrations were among Darley's least successful.

109
F.O.C. Darley
The Deerslayer
Preliminary drawing in black ink and wash, heightened with white, for a banknote design, ca. 1860

110
Alfred Jones after F.O.C. Darley
The Jack-Knife
Steel-engraved banknote design, published by American Bank Note Co., New York, 1859

111
After F.O.C. Darley
The Deerslayer
Steel-engraved banknote design, published by American Bank Note Co., New York, ca. 1860

112
F.O.C. Darley
Winter
Drawing in graphite on tracing paper, 1871–72, for *The Illustrated Christian Weekly*, February 17, 1872

113
Hayes after F.O.C. Darley
Winter
Wood engraving for *The Illustrated Christian Weekly*, February 17, 1872

114
E. and H. T. Anthony
The Village Blacksmith (fig. 15)
The Unwilling Laborer
Repose
Emigrants Attacked by Indians
Photographs of drawings by F.O.C. Darley, ca. 1863

115
F.O.C. Darley
Indian Hunting Buffalo
Preliminary drawing in graphite for a banknote design, ca. 1853
(fig. 3)

116
After F.O.C. Darley
Indian Hunting Buffalo
Steel-engraved banknote design, published by Toppan, Carpenter & Co., 1853
(fig. 4)

117
Advertisement for Continental Bank Note Company
Illustrated with steel engravings after F.O.C. Darley and others, ca. 1866

Fig. 18. F.O.C. Darley, *Dick Swiveller and Quilp*
(from *The Old Curiosity Shop*). Drawing in black ink and wash,
heightened with white, for *Character Sketches
from the Works of Charles Dickens*
(Philadelphia: Porter & Coates, 1888) [Cat. No. 126]

Darley's last published work, in 1888, was a series of illustrations of scenes from the works of Charles Dickens. The prints were large photomechanical reproductions of highly finished drawings like this one, of *Dick Swiveller and Quilp*. According to an inscription by the artist's wife, it was Darley's last; she noted that "Mr. Darley begged that he might be allowed to finish this, the last of twelve of his greatest sketches the night before he died, but was too feeble to sign the plate, dying almost with the pencil in his hand. He wished them known as the greatest work of his life, not even excepting the plates for 'Fenimore Cooper.'"

118

The American Bank-Note Company (New York: [American Bank Note Company], 1869)

119

F.O.C. Darley

Surveyors

Preliminary drawing in graphite for a bank-note design, ca. 1853

120

James Smillie after F.O.C. Darley

Surveyors

Steel-engraved banknote design, published by Toppan, Carpenter & Co., 1853

121

F.O.C. Darley

Freedom for the Slaves

Preliminary drawing in graphite for a bank-note design, 1863

122

F.O.C. Darley

[*Wood Carver*]

Preliminary drawing in graphite for a bank-note design, 1866

123

After F.O.C. Darley

[*Wood Carver*]

Steel-engraved banknote design, published by Continental Bank Note Co., 1866

124

F.O.C. Darley

The Death

Drawing in graphite, heightened with white, for Elizabeth Barrett Browning, *The Rhyme of the Duchess May*, ca. 1887

125

F.O.C. Darley

Mrs. Gargery on the Ram-page (from *Great Expectations*)

Drawing in black ink and wash, heightened with white, for *Character Sketches from the Works of Charles Dickens* (Philadelphia: Porter & Coates, 1888)

126

F.O.C. Darley

Dick Swiveller and Quilp (from *The Old Curiosity Shop*)

Drawing in black ink and wash, heightened with white, for *Character Sketches from the Works of Charles Dickens* (Philadelphia: Porter & Coates, 1888)

(fig. 18)

Selected Bibliography

"Felix O. C. Darley." *The National Magazine*, September 1856, pp. 193–97.

Sketches of Distinguished American Authors Represented in Darley's New National Picture Entitled Washington Irving and His Literary Friends at Sunnyside. New York: Irving Publishing Co., 1863.

Henry T. Tuckerman. *Book of the Artists.* New York, 1867, pp. 471–76.

Felix Octavius Carr Darley. *Sketches Abroad with Pen and Pencil.* New York, 1868.

Biographical Sketches of Benson J. Lossing, L.L.D., Author, and Felix O. C. Darley, Artist, of Our Country, A Household History for All Readers. New York: Johnson & Miles, [1876].

Frank Weitenkampf. "Illustrated by Darley." *The International Studio*, March 1925, pp. 445–48.

Frank Weitenkampf. "F.O.C. Darley, American Illustrator." *Art Quarterly*, 10 (Spring 1947): 110–13.

Theodore Bolton. "The Book Illustrations of Felix Octavius Carr Darley." *Proceedings of the American Antiquarian Society* (April 1951). Reprinted separately 1952.

Princeton University Library. *Early American Book Illustrators and Wood Engravers, 1670-1870: A Catalogue of a Collection of American Books Illustrated for the Most Part with Wood Cuts and Wood Engravings.* 2 vols. Princeton, 1958–68.

William H. Griffiths. *The Story of the American Bank Note Company.* New York: American Bank Note Company, 1959.

Ethel King. *Darley, the Most Popular Illustrator of His Time.* Brooklyn, N.Y.: Theo. Gaus' Sons, Inc., [1964].

John C. Ewers. "Not Quite Redmen: The Plains Indian Illustrations of Felix O. C. Darley." *The American Art Journal*, 3 (Fall 1971): 88–98.

Delaware Art Museum. "*. . . Illustrated by Darley*": *An Exhibition of Original Drawings by the American Book Illustrator Felix Octavius Carr Darley.* Wilmington: Delaware Art Museum, 1978.

Francis B. Dedmond. *Sylvester Judd.* Boston: Twayne Publishers, [1980], pp. 85–86.

Sue W. Reed. "F.O.C. Darley's Outline Illustrations." *The American Illustrated Book in the Nineteenth Century*, ed. Gerald W. R. Ward. Winterthur, Del.: Henry Francis Du Pont Winterthur Museum, [1982].

David E. E. Sloane. *The Literary Humor of the Urban Northeast, 1830-1890.* Baton Rouge and London: Louisiana State University Press, 1983.

Thomas Bangs Thorpe. *A New Collection of Thomas Bangs Thorpe's Sketches of the Old Southwest*, ed. David C. Estes. Baton Rouge and London: Louisiana State University Press, 1984.

Georgia B. Barnhill. "F.O.C. Darley's Illustrations for Southern Humor." Pp. 31–63 in *Graphic Arts and the South*, ed. Judy L. Larson. Fayetteville: University of Arkansas Press, 1993.

Georgia B. Barnhill. "Felix Octavius Carr Darley." Pp. 60–67 in *American Book and Magazine Illustrators to 1920*, ed. Steven E. Smith, Catherine A. Hastedt, and Donald H. Dyal. Detroit: Gale Research, 1998.